C000224667

Yorkshire Seaside Resorts and Harbours

in old picture postcards

by Vera Chapman

European Library ZALTBOMMEL/THE NETHERLANDS

GB ISBN 90 288 6482 2

© 1997 European Library – Zaltbommel/The Netherlands

No part of this book may be reproduced in any form, by print, photoprint, microfilm or any other means, without written permission from the publisher.

Introduction

These pictures of resorts and harbours of the Yorkshire coast stir happy memories of seaside holidays at their zenith such as our parents and grandparents used to enjoy and perhaps we ourselves as children. The pictures are arranged as a journey from Bridlington to Redcar, calling at places as they used to be, mainly between the 1880s and the 1930s. We shall find out a little of how each evolved and what life was like for residents and visitors in those busy times, when travel for most meant the train or bus.

The Yorkshire coast is beautiful, dramatic and varied. Its rocky cliffs are often sheer, and rise to over 600 feet in places. Even the clay cliffs at either end seem imposing as the relentless sea bites at their feet. Yet rocky headlands shelter winding creeks and sweeping bays as sandy as anyone could desire.
The qualities of the coast are recognised officially by its designations as National Park, Long Distance Footpath and Heritage Coast. They are recognised unofficially by the number of haunts which drew visitors in the days before cars and planes tempted people to go farther afield, to sunnier climes and to the ends of the earth.
The official designations have perhaps also changed our perceptions of what was at times and in places a working industrial coast. Most coastal settlements were for fishing, and the harvest

of the sea included shoals of herring and Arctic whales. But the rocks themselves provided the raw materials for local industry, mining and quarrying for alum, jet, ironstone, cement and building stone. At times parts of the coast were aflame with kelp and heather burning, alum roasting, lime burning and iron smelting.

The Yorkshire coast was also a treacherous one. At one extreme beset by the 'haar', sea fret or fog, at the other by vicious north-east gales, and, with reefs awaiting, it was a graveyard for ships. Even the largest harbours were small and often silted, unsuitable as harbours of refuge. Six Victorian piers succumbed to the waves, as did many houses, when the cliffs beneath them crumbled away.
The early villages were away from the shore. Not until later did fishing settlements emerge, but few had a formal harbour, using a creek or shore to beach their boats. Those with a harbour or quay remained of modest scale such that, untrammelled by train rails or trucks, the harbour could be one of the attractions for latter day visitors.

It was the railway that really opened up the resorts for a wider clientele. From the mid-19th century railways reached the Yorkshire coast from each end. Finally and as late as 1883, the chal-

lenging but highly scenic central stretch joined the two ends between Whitby and Loftus. Thus the Yorkshire seaside resorts became the mecca for mass tourism, serving the industrial towns of the West Riding, Teesside and Lancashire.
Yet the resorts emerged with their own characteristics. Some remained small and quiet. Some lost out when the coastal railway closed. Some with perceived potential never achieved it. Others attacted huge crowds. Many had mineral springs, but only a few developed a spa. Spa and sea water for health soon evolved into bathing, the beach and entertainments for fun. The seaside holiday had arrived.

My thanks are due to all those previous writers, too numerous to name, who have extended my knowledge and love of the Yorkshire coast and to those who have allowed me to copy their postcards and answered my queries: Kenneth Chapman, Gordon Hollis, Alan Suddes, Pamela Thomas and Darlington Borough Museum.
Many of the postcards lack a producer's name. I have acknowledged those that have, and thank the firms who gave permission.

1 This picture of Princes Parade at Bridlington Quay shows the promenade and gardens north of the harbour. Five miles of firm, level sands provide safe bathing and views of Flamborough Head where the rocky cliffs of Yorkshire begin. Bridlington had a split personality. Old Bridlington (or Burlington), the Priory and market town, lies a mile inland; the harbour known as Bridlington Quay developed as a popular family seaside resort. From the 1770s chalybeate waters emerging near the harbour gave rise to a spa around which lodgings grew up. The waters 'resembled those of Scarborough' but were 'less purgative'. By the 1820s 'great numbers of genteel people' resorted in summer for sea bathing. The coastal railway of 1846 brought a wider clientele. The track separated old and new Bridlington until the gap was built over and the two merged. (Posted 1908.)

2 The harbour, the hub of Bridlington's sea front, divides the sands into north and south. North Pier, seen here about the turn of the century, made a pleasant promenade for viewing the bay and ships. The harbour dates back to the days of the Priory. After frequent rebuildings, the timber piers were replaced in stone in 1812 under the direction of engineer John Rennie. North Pier took its present form in 1843 and South Pier in 1850. Said to be of Priory stones, they enclose a basin of 12 acres. The harbour dried out at low water, and a freshwater ebbing and flowing well appeared in its midst. The Gypsy Race stream helped to clear the silt. Ships were built until about 1840. Trade was mainly coastwise, in farm produce to London, cattle and horses to the continent, coal from the Tyne and timber from the Baltic. Fishing and general trade continued.

3 Bridlington harbour is viewed here from the end of North Pier in the 1920s or 1930s, the activities around it being a main attraction. Bridlington was by then a fully developed seaside resort catering for day-trippers and fortnightly holidaymakers. Pleasure craft took visitors on trips around the bay and Flamborough Head. Cobles provided line fishing. The fishing fleet came in and fisherman sold haddock, cod, plaice, mackerel and shellfish on stalls near the harbour. Bathing machines and warm and cold seawater baths had given way to beach chalets and donkey rides. Entertainment could be had at the Spa Theatre, the Grand Pavilion and the Floral Pavilion. In 1934 the Borough Council bought Sewerby Hall and grounds to the north for an art gallery, museum and park. It was opened by Amy Johnson, famous for her exploit in 1930 in a Gypsy Moth, the first solo flight to Australia by a woman.

THE HARBOUR, BRIDLINGTON.

4   The Priory and old town, formerly ruled from the Priory, were also attractions for discerning visitors. This picture of Bayle Gate, the gatehouse to Bridlington Priory from the town, was sent to Edward Wooler, a Darlington solicitor and antiquarian. Bayle Gate, built in 1388, stands beside Quay Road on the edge of Church Green close to Kirkgate. The west side has separate arches for carriages and pedestrians. The oak-beamed upper room served successively as the prior's court room, a prison under Cromwell, a non-conformist chapel after the Restoration, a soldiers' lodging in Napoleonic times, a 19th-century school and now a museum. From the gatehouse, the narrow High Street with its 16th-century Olde Star Inn leads to Market Place, where the stocks and pillory have been rebuilt.

(Courtesy of Fine Art Developments plc. Posted 1905.)

5 Of great appeal to visitors past and present, the Priory Church adjoining the old town dated from 1160 AD. The former nave and fragments of the cloister are the sole remnants of the 12th-century Augustinian Priory. John of Bridlington, Prior for seventeen years in the 14th century, was buried behind the high altar and later canonised as a saint. The last Prior resisted the Dissolution, joined the Pilgrimage of Grace and was executed at Tyburn in 1537. The remnant of the monastic church became this splendid parish church of St. Mary, restored in mid-Victorian times by Sir George Gilbert Scott. (Posted 1905.)

Bridlington, The Priory Church.

6   Bridlington made a convenient centre for exploring Flamborough Head, where the Yorkshire Wolds reach the sea. The chalk begins suddenly at Sewerby. The near vertical cliffs have an unusual profile, being capped by gentler slopes of boulder clay. Viewed here across Selwicks Bay, the bedding and jointing encouraged erosion into caves, stacks, natural arches and blow-holes, curiosities to the holiday-maker. Of interest to Edwardian geologists and naturalists were sponge fossils, contorted strata at Old Dor, and seabirds nesting in their thousands on Bempton cliffs, where harder chalk rises to a sheer 300 feet. The Flamborough lighthouse of 1806 in the picture replaced the nearby light tower of 1674, which signalled from a cresset or fire basket fuelled by coal. More recently, refreshments became available at the chalk- and brick-built village.

FLAMBOROUGH HEAD AND LIGHTHOUSE.

7   North Landing and South Landing lie on either side of Flamborough Head. Coble fishermen could keep a boat at each to launch according to wind and weather. Traditional cobles were based on Viking longboats. Of larch, with oak ribs, they were launched from the beach on runners or skids near the stern, and drawn back by horse or winch or simply manhandled. Stable in rough seas, they were wide, flat-bottomed and without a keel, the base being a solid baulk of timber. The clinker-built sides formed a high pointed prow and a straight stern. Some villages, as at Filey, built a pointed stern for backward rowing through the surf of a gently sloping beach. Trips for fishing, scenery and birds went from North Landing, and a lifeboat station is seen here. Some caves around 1920 still contained boulder-clay, suggesting that this small cove had been formed before the Ice Age.

IMBOROUGH.—THE NORTH LANDING

8   Old Filey village lay a little way inland. Craftsmen, traders and fishing families were centred at the north end around Queen Street, near Coble Landing where fish was brought in and sold. There is no harbour. Turnpike travellers used to visit the four inns and sample the chalybeate spring on Carr Naze, but no spa arose. New Filey emerged during the 19th century as a quiet seaside resort built on two levels. The imposing white Georgian-style hotels and boarding houses of The Crescent fronted by Crescent Gardens began in the 1830s. Down below, Victorian houses were built on Foreshore Road with a promenade seen here in the 1920s. Though boosted by the railway from 1857, the resort itself remained confined between Martins and Church Ravines. The open-top tourer AJ4710 was perhaps a Model T or Chevrolet. (Kingsway.)

S 14856   The Promenade, Filey

9 Filey Promenade and gardens are seen here from the north. There were few access points to the sea front. The sands curve for six miles between the rocks of Filey Brigg and the chalk cliffs of Speeton and Bempton. In between, in the distance, the Vale of Pickering ends in low cliffs of stiff clay eroding with the onslaught of winter gales. Minor royalty came to stay at sedate Filey, and uniformed Edwardian nannies with their young charges are remembered. Filey has managed to retain much of its Victorian and Edwardian elegance. (Posted 1934.)

The Promenade, Filey.

10   Church Ravine leads to the beach at the north end of Filey. Until 1889, when Filey became a borough, the ravine formed part of the boundary between the North and East Ridings of Yorkshire. St. Oswald's parish church founded by Bridlington Priory was built on the opposite bank from the village, in a different county! In recent times a bridge had linked the two. In the early 19th century the ravine was bare. A stream ran down to the sea and springs supplied water until piped water arrived. In 1869 the local authority bought the ravine, planted the woods and made ornamental walks. It also culverted the stream and built the road which leads to Coble Landing where, in the 1890s, were 64 inshore cobles and many larger yawls supported by seagoing cobles. (Posted 1908.)

The Ravine, Filey.

4213. 4.

11 'The Queen of English Watering Places', Scarborough, is Yorkshire's largest seaside resort. It expanded from its Norman castle, town and harbour with the discovery in 1626 of medicinal water at the cliff foot in South Bay. The Spa patronised by the gentry was followed from the 1720s by sea-water drinking and sea bathing from tents, machines and boats, a health treatment boosted by George III. The arrival of the railway from York in 1845 ushered in the modern era of mass holidays and entertainment, seaside promenades and the creation of paths and gardens along the steep clay cliffs. The southern approach brought visitors to the Belvedere and Italian Gardens above the bathing pool of 1914, and to South Cliff Gardens, Café and Bungalows. This card features the popular Café with the Bungalow roofs below. Beyond are the Tower and Spa. Above is the Prince of Wales Hotel on the Esplanade. (Posted 1922.)

Café South Cliff Gardens, Scarborough

12   South Side Bungalows gave easy access to the beach. The Café entrance porch is above, up the cliff. The Prince of Wales Hotel, aloft on the corner of the Esplanade and Prince of Wales Terrace, was built as a terrace of houses in 1850 and became a hotel about ten years later. It closed in the 1980s and is now luxury apartments. Two cars visible in the trees are the South Cliff Tramway built in 1874 by the efforts of the hotel manager. Operated by counter-balancing seawater tanks, it is the oldest of the town's five cliff tramways. One has gone, another is now closing. Beside the Spa buildings, the tall Observation Tower, built by Sir Joseph Paxton about 1860, was demolished in 1923. Between this and the Bungalows came in 1925 the concrete Arcade below the Ballroom, now a Promenade Lounge, Ocean Room and Banqueting Suite. (Wray, Scarborough.)

SOUTH SIDE BUNGALOWS & SPA, SCARBOROUGH

13   Having recently created Clarence Gardens, Alexandra Gardens and Peasholm Park in North Bay, Scarborough Council in 1912 bought an extra quarter mile of the South Bay cliffs. Harry Smith, the Borough Engineer from 1879 until 1933 who was responsible for making most of the borough's parks and gardens, landscaped the new part of the South Bay cliffs into an intricate network of shaded walks with shelters, seats and arbours. Here he created the Belvedere Gardens, the Rose Garden and sunken Italian Garden, the latter an oasis amongst the woods, fashioned into staircased terraces, with a pagoda at the top and a pool, fountain and garden at the base. The beautification of the cliffs of both bays was now virtually complete.
(Dainty Series.)

ITALIAN TERRACES, BELVEDERE GARDENS, SCARBOROUGH

14 An earlier Italian Terrace of more formal design had been created as part of a Spa redevelopment about 1858, when Sir Joseph Paxton designed the ornate Spa buildings, Swiss Cottage and criss-cross cliff pathways leading from Cliff Bridge to the Spa. This Italian Terrace adjoining the Spa on the south side was gas-lit, with a shelter at the top and a bandstand below. The stone vases and ornate iron railings have gone, as has the diamond flower bed. The lamps are now plain globes, the forecourt has been enlarged and a new bandstand below enhances an enlarged arena. (L. E. Seymour, Scarborough.)

Italian Terrace, Scarborough.

15 The Spa began in 1826 when gossipy Mrs. Farrar found that mineral springs which stained the rocks brown could provide a medicinal drink. Early facilities were primitive. The first cistern was built in 1698, but overwhelmed by a landslip in 1737. A wooden spa was destroyed by a storm in 1836. A castellated Gothic Saloon designed by Henry Wyatt was opened in 1839 and enlarged in 1847, spa water by then being an adjunct to entertainment. By 1858 came Sir Joseph Paxton's Spa redevelopment and landscaping, but his Grand Hall was destroyed by fire in 1876. The fourth Spa, of French Baroque style as in the two pictures, was an enlargement by Verity and Hunt in 1879, with a cast-iron Grand Hall for 3,000, theatre, picture gallery, restaurant, colonnaded promenade and sea wall. The North Well, chalybeate and tonic, and the South Well, salt, purgative and more generally curative, were by then minor attractions in an underground pump room beneath a bandstand.

ARBOROUGH: SPA PROMENADE.

16 Two bandstands, at either end of the main Spa complex, are shown in pictures 15 and 16. In the foreground, the straight promenade wall and pretty bandstand at the foot of Paxton's Italian Terrace gave way in 1913 to a new, more solid, classical bandstand and glass-screened seating enclosure. The promenade and sea wall were curved out to accommodate this new development designed by Sir Edwin Cooper. The far bandstand, or North Orchestra, of 1875 had been built over the Pump Room which housed the ornate North and South Wells down 22 white marble steps. For long upstaged as a spa by Harrogate, Scarbor-

ough's tiled Pump Room was in use until 1909, with a short-lived revival from 1925. In 1931, however, the bandstand was demolished, and the stairway blocked off beneath a glass kiosk, which

in turn succumbed in 1980 in favour of a roundabout. (Valentines.)

Spa Promenade, Scarborough

17 Opened in 1827 by a private company, the Cliff or Spa Bridge greatly improved access from the town to the Spa for visitors on foot. The deep Ramsdale valley separated the two, and neither Foreshore Road nor the Promenade had yet been made. This iron bridge leading from St. Nicholas' Cliff soared about 70 feet on stone pillars. A 6d toll was charged to cross the bridge and enter the spa grounds. By 1890 the toll was $^1/_2$d. Tolls lasted until 1951, when Scarborough Council bought the bridge and abolished the tolls and toll booths. Meanwhile in 1860 the Ramsdale valley had become The People's Park. The lower parts of the lofty bridge pillar were incorporated in 1875 into an oriental style People's Palace and Aquarium beneath the Valley Road. Unsuccessful even with exhibitions, concerts and a skating rink, it became an underground car park. Just beside the left-hand toll booth, a cliff tramway with a 1 in 1 slope was built in 1929.

SCARBOROUGH SPA BRIDGE & SANDS

18   Taken from the Prince of Wales Hotel, this picture shows the cliff-top Esplanade above the Spa and Paxton's maturing gardens. On the left is The Terrace, the Crown Hotel with its lofty portico at its centre. The railed gardens indicate a second terrace. Built in the 1840s, they harked back to the Regency style and gave rise to Scarborough's nickname 'The Brighton of the North'. Development on the South Cliff was accelerated by the building of the Spa's Gothic Saloon in 1839 and the arrival of the railway in 1845. Access to the South Cliff was improved when the Valley Bridge was built in 1865. The curious ceremony of the Church Parade lasted until the outbreak of the First World War. Ladies and gentlemen in their Sunday best clothes would stroll up and down the Esplanade after church, the ladies in their large hats and often with parasols too. (Valentines.)

Church Parade from Prince of Wales Hotel, Scarborough

19   This view from the Spa grounds south of Cliff Bridge shows the position of the main beach, the harbour and the old town on the neck of land behind the Norman castle. Sea bathing soon outstripped spa waters as a health cure. Settrington's print of Scarborough in 1735 is thought to be the first recording of bathing machines. A Scarborough print of 1745 shows that low wheels had given way to larger ones for more discreet bathing in deeper water, but still naked. Telescopes led to ladies covering themselves neck to ankle in flannel costumes. The men went farther out in boats with a dressing roof. 'Dippers' ensured their clients a good, quick dunking and themselves a good turnover! Seawater drinking was part of the cure. The sea as fun came later. South beach had pierrots, ice cream carts, a performing bear and dogs and Punch and Judy. Drives in horse-drawn carriages, waggonettes and charabancs were popular.

20 The Grand Hotel took five years to build. Completed in 1867, it dominates the South Bay. At the time it was believed the largest in Europe, with twelve floors, 365 rooms, 260 bedrooms and a massive lounge and grand staircase. Designed by Cuthbert Broderick, its four domes represent the four seasons. On its site, Anne Bronte died at No. 2 St. Nicholas' Cliff in 1849. Foreshore Road was completed in 1877 and Sandside by the harbour became Scarborough's Golden Mile. Bathing huts line the promenade. Below the Grand Hotel, Arcadia opened in 1903. Catlin of South Shore Pierrots bought and demolished it in 1909 for his own Arcadia.

Now the Futurist Theatre is on the site. Olympia opened in 1903 as the Fisheries Exhibition and burned down about 1970. Distant St. Mary's parish church was damaged during the Civil War. Its chancel, north transept and west towers are missing, but the rest survives.

(Boots Cash Chemists.)

21　St. Nicholas' House on the cliff top was built in the 1840s for the Scarborough banker John Woodall. It was built in Jacobean style by Henry Wyatt, designer also of the Spa's Gothic Saloon. The house and garden were bought in 1898 by Scarborough Council. Harry Smith, the Borough Engineer, added a matching new east wing for a council chamber and offices completed in 1903. He also redisigned St. Nicholas' Gardens, opened to the public in 1900. The ramp-like paths are now rustically fenced, the teardrop lamps are plain and the palm trees and pinnacles of the shelter have gone.

Queen Victoria's statue in the gardens is the only public statue in the town. Behind the photographer is St. Nicholas' Cliff Tramway, 1881, by the Central Tramway Company (Scarborough) Ltd. Steam operation has changed to electric, and the new cars of 1973 still operate.

ST. NICHOLAS GARDENS SCARBORO

22 'Rough Sea, South Bay, Scarborough' shows why harbours and fishing villages on the Yorkshire coast were tucked where possible into the north corner of a bay behind a sheltering headland. The town's station and main street, Newborough, had been connected directly to the harbour and sands by a new street, Eastborough, in 1862. Foreshore Road was completed in 1877, connecting Eastborough to the new Aquarium below Cliff Bridge (picture number 17). Trams ran along the sea front from 1904 until 1931. Note the gas lamps.
(Wherrits, Scarborough. Posted 1908.)

23 This 'View from Light-house Pier' shows the Grand Hotel, cliff tramway, St. Nicholas' Gardens and the new Town Hall (picture number 21) on the cliff, followed below by shops and entertainments on Foreshore Road. Numerous small boats line the water's edge. Boats for pleasure and for line fishing in the bay for whiting, plaice, brill and flounders were available on the beach for hire. Tunny fishing became active in the 1930s. Beach entertainers included fortune tellers, minstrels, pierrots, acrobats and preachers. Photographers roamed for customers, sand modellers performed, and donkey rides were not only for children. Shellfish stalls and harbour activities were also attractions.
(Hartmann. Posted 1904.)

Scarborough.

View from Lighthouse Pier.

24　This card, 'A Peep out of the Harbour', was a painting by Frank Mason. The harbour of 1292 had declined by Tudor times, but survived on coal trade, fishing and whaling. Redevelopment in Georgian times saw the old or middle pier lengthened by Vincent in 1732. The west or inner pier of 1820 was lengthened in 1879. The immense east or outer pier was completed about 1817 with convict labour after decades of work. The brazier lighthouse of 1804 on Vincent's Pier was raised and domed in 1840, bombarded in 1914 and rebuilt in 1931. The old inner harbour housed cargo boats and the fishing fleet, with the fish market on the west quay. Crowds watched the blessing of the boats. The North Wharf was made in 1926. Until the 1930s up to 400 seasonal herring boats came. Scottish lasses gutted and barrelled.

The outer east harbour housed yachts and pleasure boats. Paddle steamers plied from about 1880 until 1910. (Posted 1904.)

SCARBOROUGH.-A PEEP OUT OF THE HARBOUR.

25 The ancient harbour reached to where Quay Street now runs behind Sandside, but silted up. Shipyards occupied the seafront until wooden ships gave way to iron. Picturesque Sandside warehouses were cleared in 1902 for an approach to the Marine Drive being built round Castle Hill. Three ancient houses remain. No. 2 Quay Street and The Three Mariners' Inn are timber-framed. Richard III House on Sandside has an Elizabethan exterior enclosing a medieval house of about 1350, probably the home of Peter Percy, the first mayor. Richard III as Lord High Admiral often visited Scarborough before and during his reign of 1483-1485, reputedly staying here and at the castle. The house became a museum from 1914, a restaurant from 1964 and a House of Mystery museum from 1989. It has also housed Missions to Seamen and a smithy.

26 A link between Scarborough's North and South Bays was proposed as early as the 1860s. North Bay development was slow and less successful. A tunnel under the castle and a seafront road were suggested, both large undertakings. The Royal Albert Drive along the foot of North Bay cliffs was already completed by 1890. The Marine Drive round the foot of Castle Hill was begun in 1897 and not completed until 1908, being hampered by fierce storms. Tolls were charged on both vehicles and pedestrians, and ended only in 1950. The South Toll House remains at the end of Sandside. The picture shows piledriving at the southern end, where the gleaming new sea wall joins up with the East Pier of the harbour.

27   This card shows the walk from the North Cliff to the castle on the headland 300 feet above the sea. A moat protected the landward side where the main buildings were sited. The Norman castle on the site of a Roman signal station was built by William le Gros about 1130 AD, and the massive keep 100 feet tall in the innermost bailey about 1160. The Queen's Tower was named after Richard III's wife Anne Neville. During the Civil War the castle was defended by Sir Hugh Cholmley, who surrendered when supplies ran out and retired to Whitby. The Parliamentary troops were stationed at the parish church. Both castle and church were damaged by cross fire from cannon. The castle was subsequently slighted, ending its power as a fortress. It was also bombarded from the sea in the First World War. Its ruins and site are still impressive to visitors.
(Posted 1928.)

The Castle, Scarborough.

28 North Bay lagged behind South Bay, being opened up mainly in the present century. Its early private attractions had been unsuccessful. The Warwick Revolving Tower of 1897 was demolished in 1907. Rock Gardens were lost in a landslip. The ironwork North Pier, opened in 1869, was failing despite an added shopping arcade. It was destroyed by a storm in 1905. The Council had already by 1890 protected the eroding cliff with Clarence Gardens and the Royal Albert Drive. After the Marine Drive link of 1908 came a North Bay development programme. Tuckers Field was transformed in 1912 into the Japanese-style Peasholm Park.

North Bay Promenade and Bungalows beyond Peasholm Gap were followed in the 1920s and 1930s by Peasholm Glen, Northstead Manor Gardens, the Open Air Theatre, Cliff Tramway, Miniature Railway, Zoo, Swimming Pool, Corner Café and Scalby Mills, all remembered by thousands of visitors. (Valentines.)

North Bay and Bungalows, Scarborough

29   Alexandra Gardens had been laid out in 1908 on Scarborough's North Cliff at Peasholm Gap near the ends of Queens Parade and Royal Albert Drive. There were bowling greens and tennis courts. An open air stage with a semicircle of seats was covered over in 1910 as shown in this picture which was posted in 1911. A long canopy over the pavement sheltered patrons entering horse-drawn carriages. There were concert parties and pierrots. The Fol-de-Rols played there from 1911 until the 1960s. From then, famous entertainers including Arthur Askey and Jack Warner performed there. The Floral Hall was demolished in 1987. (Rotary Series. Posted 1911.)

30 On the south corner of Robin Hood's Bay, the Peak cliffs soar to an almost sheer 600 feet above the sea. Here perches Raven Hall begun by a Captain Child in 1774. Then Dr. Willis, physician to George III, lived in it and treated the ailing king here. The hall became a hotel in 1896, when the estate was sold to a West Riding development company to create a new resort, Ravenscar. A grid pattern of roads and house plots was laid out on the cliff top behind a Marine Esplanade. Despite special train trips to tempt buyers, only a few lonely plots were ever built on. Barely distinguishable tracks mark 'The Town that Never Was'. Ravenscar station on the scenic coastal railway is seen here beside a grassy square with a row of former shops. The line closed in the 1960s. Ravenscar became the terminus of the Lyke Wake Walk, and now has a National Trust centre near the former Stoup Alum Works in the bay.

31   This charming Edwardian picture by Geoffrey Hastings illustrated Robin Hood's Bay in Kendall and Wroot's 'Geology of Yorkshire'. The white line behind the lady was the old bay road near which was the gantry at which alum from Peak Alum works (1615-1862) was shipped. There were two alum works in the upper recesses of the amphitheatre of cliffs. Stoup Brow (see quarry in picture 32) worked from 1752 until 1817. Alum shales were quarried, burned in clamps, soaked and crystallised into alum mainly used for fixing dyes into woollen cloth and tanning leather. The alum industry ended in the 1870s, having lasted off and on along the Yorkshire Coast and Cleveland Hills for three centuries. The inner part of the sweeping bay is eroding masses of boulder clay left after the Ice Age, cut by streams into deep gullies, as at Boggle Hole watermill and Youth Hostel. At low tide can be seen the remnants of a dome of Jurassic rocks eroded into semi-circular scars.

32 Picturesque Robin Hood's Bay, or Bay Town, clusters along Kings Beck in a maze of steep alleyways. It began in the 15th century for fishing. 22 houses were lost to the sea in Elizabeth's reign, and Upper King Street fell in 1780. New Road then became the main street. The former Bay Hotel and 193 houses were lost during the last 200 years. A strong sea wall was built in 1975. The Dock is just a slope where fishing boats were pulled up and Whitsun Fairs held. Until the close of the 19th century fishing was the main livelihood. 130 fishermen worked five large boats and 35 cobles, rivalling Whitby and Scarborough. Boys mended nets.

Women baited the lines and barrelled the fish sent to local and Whitby markets, York, the Midlands and London. But with no harbour, larger boats could not be used, and fishing faded. Smuggling had used a network of passageways, tunnels and cellars. Adjoining houses had false cupboards.

33 Bay Town expanded up the Bank with New Town and Mount Pleasant, especially after the coastal railway arrived. Some wealthier sea captains and shipowners had already moved up. The Esplanade, Bloomswell and Martins Row pointed towards the sea and The Square, pictured here with the sign 'Mariners' Tavern'. The Square was probably an early up-town development as the inn was a haunt of smugglers with a secret tunnel in the cliff. The first school was established in two cottages in The Square in 1910. Victorian and Edwardian brick houses, hotels and villas were built on high at Mount Pleasant, near Robin Hood's Bay station, which is remembered as well kept and having flower beds and camping coaches. With the railway came artists and writers, tourists and retired people. The railway closed in 1965.

34 Whitby was famed for St. Hilda's Saxon Abbey of Streonshalh and the Synod which in 664 AD reconciled Roman and Celtic church practice. Refounded alongside in 1078, the Benedictine Abbey forms a spectacular landmark on the East Cliff beside the monks' fishpond. The ruins are those of the monastic church gradually rebuilt from 1220 over 300 years. After the Dissolution in 1536 it became ruinous. The nave, south transept and west front collapsed in turn during gales in the 18th century. The central tower collapsed in 1830. German warships did damage in 1914. Other monastic buildings entirely disappeared. The monastic abbey and town had passed to the Cholmley family, who built Abbey House nearby about 1590 with abbey stones, and added a banqueting hall circa 1680 which was ruined in a gale. The house is now a CHA holiday centre and the stables a Youth Hostel.

(Horrocks. Posted 1909.)

Whitby Abbey

35 St. Mary's parish church is unique and utterly amazing. Reached from the town by 199 steps, it lost favour with parishioners when the West Cliff was developed as a holiday resort with a new Victorian church, and was left unaltered. The Norman nave and chancel of about 1100 AD gained a tower in 1170, transepts in 1225 and 1380. The Cholmleys' pew of about 1625 on barley-sugar stilts arrongantly hid the Norman chancel arch. From about 1700 gallery after gallery was put round the interior, and the ship's deck roof and windows were built by ship's carpenters when a huge seaward extension was made in 1819. The three-decker pulpit lords it over a sea of ancient box pews seating 2,000, still warmed by an iron stove and lit by candles for occasional services.

36 The Cholmleys became Lords of the Manor of Whitby. Haggerlythe, a continuation of Kirkgate under the East Cliff, was recorded in 1270. In 1761 it was renamed Henrietta Street after Nathaniel Cholmley's wife. Subsequently most of it disappeared in cliff falls, but the Fortune family's kippering house survived, the last in Whitby and a traditional mecca for visitors. Jet from the cliffs was carved into souvenir jewellery and ornaments and one jet workshop remains intact at the foot of Church Steps. Nathaniel Cholmley in 1788 financed the new Town Hall pictured here in the Market Square in Church Street, formerly Kirkgate. Dairy produce was sold behind the pillars. A stone spiral stair led to the manor court and burgesses' meetings above. The abbey's chancel and north transept are pictured, probably before consolidation work was carried out.

37 Tin Ghaut at the Church Street end of Grape Lane was demolished in 1959 amid protest. It was one of numerous yards or ghauts behind the old streets of Whitby, from which some were entered through tunnels. Buildings crowded in at various levels, some below street level and up and down steps. Some yards, like Tin Ghaut, led down to the harbour side, others backed up to the cliffs. Many of the surviving ones have been tidied up and still have small businesses. They are a quaint survival of the old town crowded under the cliffs in the gorge of the river Esk. Arguments Yard off Church Street is well known, and still causes amusement. A local firm, Argument, owned bathing machines. Loggerhead yard went down to the harbour off Baxtergate. (J. Salmon.)

TIN GHAUT, WHITBY.

38 These galleried houses on Boulby Bank were demolished in 1958. They were on the east side of the inner harbour and behind the east side of Church Street, between Bridge Street and Green Lane, roughly opposite the railway station and Endeavour Wharf of 1965, where the whale blubber boiling houses and ship-building yards had been. They provided another sort of solution to building up the cliffs. At the foot of the cliff was Boulby's Ropery, marked on John Wood's Plan of Whitby, 1828. At the top of the Bank was the house of Sir Anthony Boulby, a noted surgeon and member of an old Whitby family. (Copyright photograph courtesy of Judges Postcards Ltd., Hastings, 01424 420919.)

39   Beside the outer harbour on the west side, Haggersgate or Hacklesougate was named in a charter of 1296. St. Ann's Staithe or Quay with houses on was built out over the water on wooden piles or staithes before 1639, but long gone except for the name. St. Ann's Lane led up to Flowergate on the west and stepping stones led across the river. The seaward end of Haggersgate used to be covered at high tide, and was raised up near the pier in the 18th century. The harbourside road leading to the Fish Quay and West Pier was widened to give more space for quayside activities. Lined with shops and stalls, it became thronged in summer. On the left are Edward's confectioners, the Red Lion and Grays. (Valentines.)

St. Ann's Staithe, Whitby

Valentine's Series

40 The herring fleet is tied up here in the inner harbour beyond the bridge, with a backdrop of buildings crowding Grape Lane and Kirkgate. The stables of Abbey House perch on the cliff above. Captain Cook's wooden expedition ships, the Whitby 'cats' or colliers designed for coastal trade, were built on the west bank, now occupied by the Endeavour Wharf built in 1965. Around the inner harbour were four boiling houses for whale blubber oil for lighting, lubricants, soap and paint. 55 Whitby ships made 577 Arctic whaling voyages over an eighty-year period. The Whitby Herring Company was formed in 1833 to cure herrings and other fish for home and export. Scottish herring boats and fisher lasses used to follow the shoals of herrings, nicknamed silver darlings, down the east coast as far as Yarmouth.
(Valentines.)

Herring Fleet Unlading, Whitby

41 Fishing boats are shown here by the quayside in Whitby's outer harbour, probably about the turn of the century, when sail was not yet replaced by motor boats. Fishing boats were numerous from the 14th century, paying dues to the Abbey. The difficult entrance to the outer harbour was protected by a series of piers built out into the sea. Timber ones were recorded in 1545. These were rebuilt in stone and timber by Sir Hugh Cholmley in 1632, and in stone in the 18th and early 19th century when the final extensions were made. The lighthouses were built in 1814 and 1854. High on the West Cliff is the Royal Hotel in the new resort founded by George Hudson, when his Pickering to Whitby railway arrived in 1847. This tinted card was produced by Horne and Son, Abbey Press, Whitby. They were printers and publishers of the Whitby Gazette and Visitors' List from 1854. The newspaper is still in production.

Fishing Boats in Harbour, W...

42 Postcards of Whitby scenes edged with gilt borders and a green surround with gilded patriotic symbols were produced by Raphael Tuck and Sons. This shows a paddle steamer passing Tate Hill Pier near Burgess Pier at the foot of Church Steps. Trips could be taken around Whitby Bay or to Scarborough. In the background the landslips which carried away much of Henrietta Street appear as raw scars on the left. A chalybeate spring in East Cliff reached by a ladder and baths at the foot were also destroyed. Much of East Cliff consists of crumbly shales with a layer of jet rock at the base at tide level. Jet was worked in 200 workshops until 1890 and, farther round the cliff, alum shales were worked at Saltwick Nab until 1821. Both industries added to the prosperity of Whitby as a seafaring town which had over 1,000 seamen.

(Courtesy of Fine Art Developments plc.)

WHITBY, THE EAST CLIFF.

43 At Ruswarp, the first village up the river Esk from Whitby harbour and station, the Boat Landing was a pleasant spot for visitors. A cattle market and a flour mill served the local area, and the mill weir and dam allowed rowing boats for pleasure near Ruswarp station, as shown in this card. The mill was recently turned into flats. (Brittain & Wright. Posted 1905.)

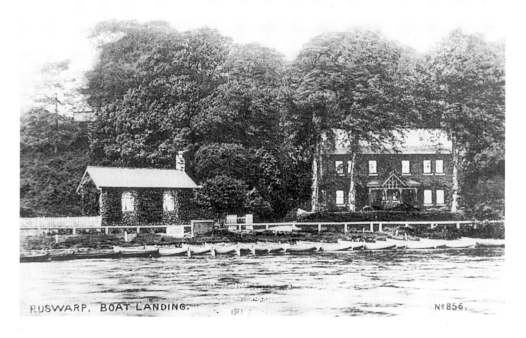

RUSWARP. BOAT LANDING.   No 856.

44 Visitors to Whitby could also follow footpaths inland along Eskdale to beauty spots, including Golden Grove, Falling Foss waterfall and Sleights, or by railway to Goathland and the waterfall Mallyon Spout. Some footpaths were flagged. From Ruswarp popular footpaths led along the wooded Rigg Mill Beck to Rigg Mill, where there was a ford. Rigg Mill could also be reached from Hawsker station on the coastal railway.

(Copyright photograph courtesy of Judges Postcards Ltd., Hastings, 01424 420919.)

11590. NR. WHITBY. RIGG MILL - ROCKS W

45 Sandsend developed in a small way as a quiet holiday beach of firm sands at the north end of Whitby Bay, where Sandsend Beck and East Row Beck run parallel to the sea. Seafront houses and the modest promenade between the becks are shown in this card posted in 1910. The older houses at East Row Beck were built for alum workers. Courtesy paths led beside Sandsend Beck through woods on the Mulgrave Castle Estate, where the former castle built in 1200 AD lay in ruins. This beach no doubt became popular after the coastal railway and station arrived in 1883.

46 The coastal railway closed in 1958. The iron viaduct was demolished, but the station building remains. The railway ran north along the cliff edge via three old alum quarries and through a tunnel beyond. The present car park beside steep Lythe Bank is on the site of the boiling house of Sandsend alum works, one of the most successful on the Yorkshire coast. It operated in Mulgrave woods and cliffs from 1615 until about 1870. When Peter Spence invented a new process, the industry moved to the coalfields and the old works scooped out of the Yorkshire cliffs and Cleveland Hills died. In the upper layers of the Lias shales at Sandsend occurred lines of calcareous nodules or cement stones which were extracted until at least the 1920s to make Mulgrave Cement. The quarries are now a nature trail.

(Photograph courtesy of Judges Postcards Ltd., Hastings 01424 420919.)

23204. SANDSEND.   JUDGES' LTD

47   A long battle with its slipping cliff has ensued since 1664 when all but one house of the old village of Runswick Bay slid into the sea. Rebuilt nearby, the small, red-roofed village clings to its cliff in a jumble of cottages connected by a maze of cobbled pathways. Last century the villagers fished from twenty cobles and five yawls. Beloved of artists, it is now a holiday village. Cliff slips and falls still occur, and the winding access lane has had to be closed. A wide new road was sliced down the bay in 1962 for visitor parking by the beach. A new sea wall came in 1970. Mothers used to bring children with whooping cough to Hob Holes to plead with Hob the goblin for a cure. Kettleness headland, supported by ironstone rock at its base, was reshaped by alum quarrying between 1728 and 1871.

(Fine Art Developments plc. Posted 1907.)

PICTURESQUE YORKSHIRE. — A Sunny Afternoon at Runswick.

48   Port Mulgrave harbour was built in the 1850s in a small bay beneath a 300-foot cliff. A private harbour, it served Charles Mark Palmer's Grinkle mine three miles inland. The ironstone was conveyed in a rope-hauled tramway passing through two long tunnels to emerge on to gantries on the quay, from which hoppers discharged into ships bound for Palmer's shipyards in Jarrow on the Tyne. The mine and harbour closed in 1921, the mine already having been con-nected to the coastal railway. The port installations were removed after a severe fire. The harbour was breached during the Second World War to prevent a German landing, and again by the drastic storm of 1953. On the cliff top were the engine house, offices, Short Row and Long Row for the port workers. Palmer built for himself near the mine the mansion Grinkle Park, now a hotel.

49   Staithes huddles beside Roxby Beck as it enters the small bay between Cowbar Nab and Penny Nab. There was only a tiny quay, but boats were beached on the shore or moored up the creek behind Cowbar headland. The original village, Seaton, was inland. By the 15th century, it had been deserted for Staithes which grew to be the pre-eminent fishing village of the Yorkshire coast. At its peak there were around 300-400 fishermen and up to 120 boats. Slow decline followed the advent of steam trawlers, refrigeration, Whitby fishing fleet's revival, two World Wars and the coastal railway closure. But Staithes had other interests, and expanded inland with housing for local ironstone miners. Alum and ironstone were shipped, some jet was mined, an artist's colony grew and holiday makers and day trippers flocked by train and car. (Brittain and Wright. Posted 1911.)

STAITHES, YORKS.   No 1983.

50 The scenic coastal route was a feat of railway construction, taking many years to complete. From the 1880s, a lofty lattice girder viaduct took the railway soaring over the deep glen to Staithes station at the top of the bank. Staithes viaduct had a unique wind gauge with a bell to sound in the signal box when it was unsafe for a train to cross! Only the abutments and pillar bases remain after demolition, and the station area is now a car park. Three fish trains weekly took fish to York, Leeds, Manchester and London. Visitors came by rail from industrial Teesside, or dropped off for half a day at Staithes on their way to Whitby. The last through train between Whitby and Loftus ran in 1958.
(T. Watson, Lyth.)

51 The approach to old Staithes leads steeply down the bank from the station into High Street, where tall buildings emphasise the narrowness of the street. About six times the size of Runswick, it developed largely in the 19th century a town-like appearance, with numerous shops, a Co-op., a bank, two hotels, Wesleyan and Primitive Methodist and Bethel Congregational chapels, a Mission Room, a Roman Catholic church, a Board School and a Fisherman's Institute. Behind the frontages was a maze of passages leading to houses at higher and lower levels and to the beck and a footbridge to Cowbar.

High Street, Staithes.

52 Taking a photograph was an event which drew people's attention in the High Street, seen here in its level stretch. Victorian and Edwardian bays have been added as well as shop windows. The sharp turn leads to the sea front. Old Staithes was a tight-knit community with a few old families dominant: the Verrills, Unthanks, Theakers, Lavericks, Seekers, Coles, Roddams and Browns. A local dialect with Norse influence was spoken. Nicknames were commonly used, as Black Dick, Fancy Joe, Talking Tom and Old Dutchy.
(Posted in 1907.)

53 A labyrinth of narrow passageways, vennels or ginnels connected by flights of steps and paved or cobbled slopes, gave access to the stone and pantiled cottages piled above each other on the steep valley side. Some passages had odd names: Slip Top, Dog Loup, Stone Gap, Gun and Gutter and The Old Stubble. The ladies in the picture are wearing traditional clothing. The Staithes bonnet is of a design special to Staithes, with a long poke and a frilled back flap, and is still worn by some ladies for visitors and special events. The man wears his guernsey or 'gansey' and perhaps blue pilot cloth trousers. Fishermen formerly wore knee breeches.

A Bit of Old Staithes

54 Looking down Staithes creek at the seaward end of Roxby Beck we see Penny Nab, the east cheek of the bay. On the left is the roadside below Cowbar Nab with its line of cottages and the lifeboat station housed from 1875 in the disused alum warehouse. The road from here leads back and steeply upwards to Cowbar and terraced houses formerly for workers at Boulby alum works on the cliffs to the north. Cobles are moored at low tide in the shelter of the Nab. Staithes cobles had the stable traditional Viking style of clinker-built sides, flat bottoms, a high pointed prow and a flat rear, yet could be carried on land by two men.

By 1950, fishing had almost died, but some inshore crab and lobster catching still goes on. In the early decades of this century Staithes became an artists' colony under the influence of Dame Laura Knight. Artists still come to paint the picturesque scenes.

55 High Street ends in a narrow approach to the short sea front and beach of Staithes beyond The Cod and Lobster public house. On the right are Barras or Barris Steps. They led to a square surrounded by houses on three sides, the only open space in closely-packed old Staithes apart from the sea front. Several paths converged on The Barras, which used to have a public pump. Was this a general meeting place where the annual Fair was held, perhaps an informal market place or a net mending space? Preparations for the Fair or Feast kept the public bakehouse busy, as few cottages had ovens. The Fair has more recently become Carnival Week.

56 The Cod and Lobster inn stood as an isolated block of buildings at the end of High Street. A small promenade behind it led pedestrians round to the sea front, sands and boat landings at Seaton Garth. The old inn buildings seen in the picture were badly damaged in the devastating east coast storm and tidal surge of 1953, and were rebuilt. Crab sandwiches are still a favourite with visitors. (Frith.)

Staithes, "The Cod and Lobster."

57 Staithes in its small bay was particularly vulnerable to the sea rather than to cliff falls. In the 18th century a whole street was washed away. William Sanderson's shop, where Captain Cook was apprenticed, went about 1812, and in 1832 thirteen houses also went. A village school was said in 1890 to have been lost to the sea 'in living memory', and the Square between rows of houses at Seaton Garth was also washed away. In 1928 a breakwater and harbour was built by the Ministry of Agriculture and Fisheries. This card entitled 'High Tide' was posted during Edward VII's reign. The waves are dashing against the buildings in the yards behind the lower part of High Street. The Cod and Lobster juts out to the left, and cottages at Seaton Garth are in the distance. (Brittain and Wright. Posted pre-1910.)

STAITHES. HIGH TIDE.

58 Entitled 'Selling the Crabs', this picture shows typical cobles drawn up on the beach, their long oars leaning against the sea wall. Out at sea, groups of three-man cobles could off-load their fish on to a five-man yawl. Nets are drying on the railings. A group of men watches the men and women below, presumably 'unlading' the catch. The women are wearing their typical white aprons and Staithes bonnets. One woman appears to have something on top of her bonnet. The women normally carried loads on their heads as the village alleyways were impossible for horses and carts, and some even for donkeys. Water from the beck, bread from the bakehouse, fish, bait and even building materials were balanced on women's heads.
(Valentines.)

" Selling the Crabs," Staithes

59 The seamen are wearing their navy blue 'ganseys' (a dialect variant of Guernseys or Jerseys), hand-knitted by the women of the family to the traditional Staithes pattern. Each fishing village had its own stitch pattern by which the provenance of fishermen could be recognised, especially after injury or drowning. Women collected flithers (limpets) for bait, baited the lines, cut up and salted fish, soaked it in brine to pickle and dry on the beach, repaired nets, launched boats and attended fish auctions. Herring, codling, mackerel and haddock, ling, turbot, crab and lobster were caught. Fifteen herring boats went off to Yarmouth in the season. (Posted 1904.)

STAITHES   A CHARACTERISTIC SCENE

60 Fishermen's cottages about the turn of the century at the far end of the bay at Seaton Garth are built up against the slope of Penny Nab. Oars are propped up on the shales and shingle. A collection of floats and nets hangs over what appears to be a winch or winding apparatus for hauling boats or nets. The bonnetted lady shows that the ground floor of the white-washed stone cottage is sunken. Her windows are of the so-called Yorkshire sash or sideways sliding sash, so typical of the area until recent times.

Fishermen's Cottages, Staithes.

2197

61 Church Street, Staithes, ran steeply down the bank parallel with High Street, but in a separate valley. It was thought to be the route to the old parish church at Hinderwell. It seems less developed than High Street, and more homely. The man wearing gaiters and carrying cans on a yoke may be a local farmer delivering milk, which was also delivered on a donkey with panniers. Another similar postcard catches women in bonnets gossiping and hens running about the street.

62 The tiny farming and fishing community in the deep Skinningrove valley was transformed from 1848 by companies mining the Main Seam of the Cleveland ironstone. By the 1890s over 700 men were employed, the Skinningrove Iron Company's works were on the cliff top, and in 1890 the company built a strong jetty far below. The Quaker company Pease and Partners mined here from 1868. They reclaimed the estuary with a sea wall and in the 1870s built for their incoming workers this model village of 200 terraced houses with two chapels, a school, a Miners' Institute and a hospital. Healthy leisure was in Timm's Coffee House, cricket, quoits, allotment gardens and pigeon crees. The men took to work a food box, a tea or coffee tin and a candle holder, and wore moleskin or fustian trousers. Mining ended in 1958. Almost all these houses were demolished. Fewer new ones with gardens have replaced them.

63 Old Saltburn nestled at Huntcliff, where the rocky cliffs of Yorkshire end. In 1861 Henry Pease extended the Stockton and Darlington Railway to serve his new genteel resort of Saltburn-by-the-Sea between the Skelton Beck and Hazel Grove. His Improvement Company provided the pier, cliff lift and 'bathing machines and attendants at all times'. From the pier, steamers plied to Hartlepool, Whitby and Scarborough. The pier, now the only survivor of six on the Yorkshire coast, was opened in 1870, but damaged by storms in 1874 and 1875. It was bought in 1880 by the Middlesbrough Estates Company and rebuilt with a bandstand, shelters, theatre and shops. Rammed by the ship 'Ovenberg' in 1924, it was reconnected in 1930, only to be partly dismantled in the Second World War. Reunited in 1947, the storms of 1953 and 1974 led to its being shortened, but still in use. (Posted 1903.)

HUNTCLIFF AND PIER.

middlesbrough 160 saltburn 226 (3 whts). I scored 6 not out.

64 At first Saltburn pier was reached from the town via a vertical rope-hauled wooden lift or hoist with a cage for twenty passengers. The lift was replaced from 1884 by this water-balanced inclined hydraulic tramway with cars for ten passengers each. A spring in the cliff fed a reservoir from which water was pumped in turn to a tank under the upper car. The early cars had red plush seating and stained glass windows. This picture was taken from the pier beyond its two entrance shops.

(Dainty Series. Posted 1912.)

65 Cat Nab, a curious hill of clay, shelters Skelton Beck, the farm with a barn and gin-gan for threshing and the stables with circular haystacks. On the right is the fishing and smuggling hamlet of old Saltburn with the Ship Inn, possibly 16th century, now a pub and restaurant. The Assembly Rooms for theatre, concerts and balls, now gone, were built in 1864 at the lower end of Skelton glen. Now there is a small fairground and stalls. Bathing machines were used near the Ship Inn until the Second World War. A children's Sand Service was held on August Bank Holidays. Motor Race Day Trials were held on the sands until 1914, and in 1922-1924 Malcolm Campbell broke the World Speed Record, but was disallowed. Seas in 1938 spoiled the sands and racing moved to Coatham sands, all to be stripped by the sea surge of 1953.

(Posted 1903.)

SALTBURN.—CAT-NAB.

66 The Zetland Hotel was opened in 1863. The centre-piece of the new resort, it was flanked by Balmoral and Britannia Terraces. The railway offloaded supplies straight into the rear of the hotel. Behind, astride the station, came a grid-iron of streets of boarding houses, glass and iron canopied shops and a group named Emerald, Ruby, Amber, Garnet, Pearl, Coral and Diamond Streets. This was Henry Pease's jewelled city, his Celestial City or New Jerusalem, also called a North Country Brighton and even The Teneriffe of the North! It was select, with quiet beaches, tolls on the pier and gardens and no public houses. After the war it became more a residential town for Teesside. The Alexandra, Queen's and Zetland Hotels were converted into apartments. The white-brick town of the 1860s now celebrates its past with a Victorian and Heritage week each August.

67 At the west end of the resort, overlooking Hazel Grove, Pease and Partners built their white brick Convalescent Home, opened in 1872 to accommodate seventy of their workers free of charge for a week. It was a particular interest of Mary Pease, Henry's wife. She used to write many letters concerning it from the sunny drawing room of their mansion 'Pierremont' in Darlington. From the mid-19th century the Peases had about a dozen ironstone mines in the Cleveland area. They had begun a convalescent home in 1867 in two cottages.

CONVALESCENT HOME. SALTBURN.

68 The Italian Gardens were Henry Pease's special creation in the Skelton Valley Gardens which 'Art has converted into a Paradise of Beauty'. Trees were planted, terraced paths and gravelled walks laid, greenhouses and a gardener's house built, and provision made for tennis and croquet. After Prince Albert died, the classical portico of Barnard Castle's first station was erected high in the gardens as the Albert Memorial of 1861. Stone sleepers from the early years of the Stockton and Darlington Railway formed steps up to the memorial. The Halfpenny Bridge, an iron girder toll bridge on cast iron columns, crossed over the gardens, but was demolished as unsafe in 1974. In a nook at the upper end of the gardens was a bubbling chalybeate spring of benefit for anaemia, stomach and skin complaints. Plants now grow in the little spa basin.

69   Upstream from the Valley Gardens visitors could continue along paths through this thick woodland beauty spot by courtesy of the Earl of Zetland. Near Rifts Wood the coastal railway from Whitby crossed the deep ravine of the Skelton Beck. Below, as seen looking downstream from the lofty viaduct, is Rifts Wood Mill or Marske Mill. The mill race ran along a rock face and under the viaduct to reach the mill and rejoin the beck, but the mill became ruinous. On the left, Rushpool Hall towers above the beck, a Victorian Gothic country house off Saltburn Lane, now a hotel. It was built for John Bell in 1863, gutted by fire in 1906 and rebuilt. Joseph Walton MP and Arthur J. Dorman, the Teesside ironmaster, have both lived there.
(Photochrom.)

2622. RIFTS WOOD MILL.

70 Although cobles were launched from the beach, Marske-by-the-Sea was mainly a farming village. The older north end of High Street, still with a cruck-framed house, grew southwards when miners, the railway and an incipient resort arrived. From the 1860s Pease and Partners built New Marske village at their Upleatham mine two miles inland. Old Marske curved off in terraced houses ending with Cliff Terrace at the beach. These houses, pictured in the 1920s, look over Spout Beck, one of many coastal gulleys or 'howles' which cut the low clay cliffs. On their brink the tower of St. Germain's, the old parish church, was kept as a landmark for ships. This rough 'howle', its stream culverted, became Valley Gardens. The former tithe barn became a grain store. The High Street was extended in 1925 as the coast road to Redcar.

(J. W. Pounder. Posted 1929.)

MARSKE-BY-THE-SEA: ZETLAND TERRACE.

71   Joseph Pease of Darlington bought Cliff Terrace, Marske-by-the-Sea, in 1844. Beyond it, perched above the beach amongst sandhills, Cliff House became his family holiday home. On a headland between Spout Beck Howle and Flat Howle, the castellated Gothic mansion was said to be built of freestone from Upleatham mine. A moat was surmounted by a sea front terrace balustraded with Pease's white bricks. Since Joseph was blind for the last seven years of his life, the 'moat' was perhaps a device for exercise without supervision. His Darlington home had a trench called 'blind man's walk'. His brother Arthur's widow and family later lived at Cliff House, then her son Claude, a noted polo player. Many visitors will remember it as a H.F. (Holiday Fellowship) Guest House. It is now sheltered housing.

72   Marske Hall on Kirkleatham Road was built near the centre of Marske in 1625 by Sir William Pennyman. Facing the busy Kirkleatham Road over open lawns, it is a well-known landmark near the shopping centre now that Marske has become a large residential area. Externally the hall had changed little. Two stone dormers had gone and the leaded windows had become sashes. Stone domes over three square towers and the Pennyman arms in a square panel mark it out. Sir William died in the Royalist cause during the Civil War. The hall and manors of Saltburn, Marske, Upleatham and Red-car were bought in the 18th century by the Dundas family of Aske, later Earls of Zetland. The hall was restored about 1900 as a summer residence for Lord and Lady Zetland between the London and shooting seasons. It is now a Cheshire Home for disabled people.

73 Redcar High Street had market stalls on both sides. The cast iron drinking fountain was wrecked by a car in 1923. The tall red lamp nearby was one of two lined up to guide ships. Now the Edward VII memorial clock tower is the focal point. There are few old buildings except at the Coatham end. Blown sand was a big problem. The old fishing village and quiet bathing resort developed rapidly after the railway came in 1846. High Street boarding houses later became shops. Before and after the First World War Redcar was in its hey-day as the holiday resort for industrial Teesside. After the Second World War industry encroached downstream towards Teesmouth. Redcar, unable to compete with cheap holidays abroad, expanded as a dormitory town with summer weekend day-trippers.
(Gem Series. Posted 1908.)

74 Redcar's sea wall and promenade were built about 1870. Horse racing and training used the beach until the racecourse opened in 1872. A Convalescent Home of 1861 expanded to take 180 patients. Redcar as a spa may have meant seawater treatments at the Hydropathic Establishment on the Esplanade. The 1890s saw N-E-R tourist rail tickets to Redcar. Excursion trains brought mass visits in workers' annual outings and trips for underprivileged children. Bathing machines and tents, sand yachting, pierrots, motor speed trials, paddle steamer trips and donkey rides are remembered from between the wars. Redcar's chief attraction, its firm sands, smooth as velvet and flat as a pancake, came right up to the promenade until 1938, when storms began to remove them. Sun City, a vast remedial marina proposed in the 1960s, was not built. (Dainty Series. Posted 1912.)

75   Piers were built at Redcar, 1871, at Redcar Lane end, and at Coatham, 1873, at Station Road end. Both piers had a chequered history. Redcar pier was struck by ships in the 1880s and 1890s and shortened, then burnt down in 1898. A pierhead pavilion and ballroom of 1907, enlarged with tearooms in 1928, must have replaced the kiosks in the picture. Cut during the Second World War, storm damage then led to demolition. The ballroom survived, but has now gone. The lifeboat museum opposite houses the Zetland, built in 1800 and retired in 1880, the world's oldest surviving lifeboat. Coatham pier was hit by two ships in its first year and shortened. Wrecked by a hit in 1898, the remnants were dismantled. The pierhead concert hall was rebuilt in the 1920s as the New Pavilion, and became the Regent Cinema in the 1960s.

Under concrete arches below was a café.
(Dainty Series. Posted 1912.)

THE PIER, REDCAR.

76 West or Salt Scar and East Scar run out from Redcar beach. A Japanese ship, the Awa Maru, was stranded on West Scar in a thunderstorm on 27 December 1906, and refloated in January. Redcar lifeboat and fishing boats saved the crew, who were accommodated in the Swan Hotel in High Street. The Yorkshire coast was a grave-yard for ships, both sail and steam, especially in north-east gales. Even Whitby, Scarborough and Bridlington were inaccessible at low tide. Despite a plan in 1832 to build a harbour of refuge in the deep water between the scars at Redcar, no harbour was ever built. To improve access to the silted estuary of the Tees, the South Gare breakwater was built between 1861 and 1888, using iron-works slag. Later slag dumping, however, in time built up an underwater reef which has affected tides and beaches.

AWA MARU ASHORE AT REDCAR DEC! 27." 1906.